Ngarla Songs

Alexander Brown
& Brian Geytenbeek

Illustrated by Jilalga Murray

Fremantle Arts Centre Press

Australia's finest small publisher

First published 2003 by
FREMANTLE ARTS CENTRE PRESS
25 Quarry Street, Fremantle
(PO Box 158, North Fremantle 6159)
Western Australia.
www.facp.iinet.net.au

Published in association with Wangka Maya Pilbara Aboriginal Language Centre.

Cover Design Adrienne Zuvela.
Internal Design Concept Jilalga Murray.
Illustrations Jilalga Murray.
Printed by Griffin Press.

National Library of Australia
Cataloguing-in-publication data

Ngarla songs.

ISBN 1 920731 73 3.

1. Aborigines, Australian - Western Australia - Pilbara - Music.
2. Aborigines, Australian - Songs and music. I. Brown,
Alexander. II. Geytenbeek, Brian. III. Murray, Jilalga.

782.421629915

The State of Western Australia has made an investment in this project through
ArtsWA in association with the Lotteries Commission.

Publication of this title was assisted by the Commonwealth Government through
the Australia Council, its arts funding and advisory body.

ATSIC

Acknowledgements

Publication of *Ngarla Songs* has relied on a number of people and organisations. First are the original singers and their families who through the Ngarla Working Group gave permission for these songs to be recorded, transcribed, translated and published. Then there is Alexander 'Sandy' Brown who knows these songs and realised the need to have them recorded. Summer Institute of Linguistics field linguist Brian Geytenbeek and Sandy Brown recorded, transcribed and translated the songs. This was a spare time project that spread over some fifteen years.

Sandy and Brian entrusted Wangka Maya Pilbara Aboriginal Language Centre (WMPALC) with bringing the songs to publication. Wangka Maya manager Fran Haintz sought and received funding from the Australia Council, and the Aboriginal and Torres Strait Islander Commission (ATSIC).

Wangka Maya graphic artist Jilalga Murray was given permission by the Ngarla Working Group to do the artwork, graphic design and layout. Sandy provided some of the photographs and illustrations. Nick Smith provided a number of photos. The Battye Library of West Australian history provided one photo. Trish Parker provided a number of pictures from which Jilalga was able to make historically accurate drawings. Wangka Maya senior linguist Albert Burgman edited the work.

Sandy Brown.

Alexander 'Sandy' Brown was born in a bough shade on De Grey Station in January 1930. As a boy he learned the Ngarla, Nyamal, and Coastal Nyangumarta languages, the niceties and intricacies of their cultures, and all the Aboriginal knowledge and skills of bush living. He also learned many station skills.

In 1949 he filled an unexpected vacancy in a droving team, taking cattle from Ethel Creek to Meekatharra. From there he caught the train south, and did seasonal work in the south-west of Western Australia.

In 1952 a man who had to drive across the Nullarbor to South Australia wanted company, so Sandy went with him. He did some seasonal work in the south-east of South Australia, went on to Melbourne, then joined a shearing team in the Australian Capital Territory. For some seventeen years he worked with that team up and down vast areas of New South Wales and Queensland, even getting as far as Normanton.

He returned to the Pilbara in 1970, worked on Mulyie Station for a while, and then worked with the Hedland Town Council until his retirement in January 1995. He learned to read and write in 1984, and has been recording aspects of his language and culture ever since.

Brian Burnet Geytenbeek was born on a farm in South Australia in 1933. He and his wife were among the founding members of the Australian Aborigines Branch of the Summer Institute of Linguistics, and were field linguists with that organisation for forty-one years. They worked with the Bandjalang people (Gidabal dialect) in New South Wales from 1962 to 1967 (where Brian also recorded some songs for a friend), and then served for some years in administration in the Field Centre in Darwin. Their last thirty years with SIL included twenty years spent in Western Australia as residents of the Tjalku Wara Aboriginal Community near Port Hedland. Their primary assignment while there was to record the Nyangumarta language, but over the years Brian assisted several other language groups with small projects when time permitted.

Jilalga Murray was born in Melbourne in 1978. Her family are of the Nyangumarta and Wamba Wamba language groups and her skin group is Karimarra. Jilalga is a talented artist and designer with two successful solo exhibitions in Port Hedland and Perth as well as a number of group exhibitions. Numerous commissions, community arts projects and publications have placed her as a leading light among talented young Aboriginal artists. Jilalga now lives in Port Hedland with her partner, daughter and dog. She is quietly enjoying her rise as an exhibiting artist and designer whose dreams are slowly coming true.

Contents

Above: De Grey Station and the cabbage gums.
Below: Walyparn Pool on Walyparn River.

Introduction

I first became aware of the wealth of descriptive and poetic material in the Ngarla language while teaching Alexander 'Sandy' Brown to read and write. At that time (1984) Sandy was in his mid-fifties. Both of us had full-time work, and the only time that we could spare for his lessons was on Saturday afternoons. There was no written Ngarla material available, so I got him to teach me the basics of the language first. From what he dictated to me — word lists, verb forms, short accounts of events in his younger years on De Grey Station, captions to photos of his many years with shearing teams in New South Wales and Queensland, and so on — I selected appropriate material, and from that he learned to read and write, using the Ngarla language as his learning medium.

He obviously knew a lot of Ngarla songs, so I transcribed several of them for him to use for reading practice. If he could not work out any particular word, he could sing the song through to that point, and identify it that way.

During that process I became aware of the wealth of emotions so skilfully expressed in the songs. I also became aware of an interesting 'staggered recycling' feature used in several of the songs. In a recycling pattern one does not sing the exact whole of any verse. Instead, the sung verses overlap (one could say, are

'staggered a few words to the right of') the written verses. The points at which recycling takes place are signalled by a tense little 'uuuiii' signal, made with lips very straight and the tongue held very close to the roof of one's mouth. Sandy, however, is able to dictate (or write down) the written form of such recycling songs without having to write down the oral form first.

When I presented him with a Certificate of Reading in 1985 I explained to him that the Aboriginal alphabet we use and the rules of pronunciation that go with it would fit any of the other Aboriginal languages he knew, so that he would now also be able to read and write in each of those languages. On his next two visits he brought me several pages containing the words of various Aboriginal songs that he had written down. There were five different languages represented in those few pages.

The particular selection from Sandy's repertoire contained in these pages has been restricted to Ngarla songs. In most cases Sandy knew the composer personally, knew the people involved in the events referred to in the song and was aware of the situation which prompted the song. In one of them he was one of the children taking part in the event described and in another he was one of a line of men involved in using fire for mustering. He was thus able to explain to me the often vague and indirect allusions which are part of the style of the songs.

If one is unaware of these indirect allusions, many of the songs are, in effect, a kind of indecipherable riddle. One has to be 'in the know' as to what is being referred to, or else the subtlety of such songs will be completely inaccessible to the listener or reader.

In more than two decades of linguistic work in another language in the Pilbara I have found very little metaphor in everyday speech, and metaphor used in English was often bewildering to the listeners. In these 'everyday' anecdotal Ngarla songs, however, metaphor is obvious in several places. (Though the Ngarla had no secret/sacred songs of their own, Sandy says metaphor is embedded in the secret/sacred songs of Nyamal and other surrounding languages. Women, girls and uninitiated boys often knew the surface meaning of the words of the songs they were allowed to hear, but did not expect to know the secret underlying meaning that the words were being used to hint at. That knowledge was reserved only for the initiated men.)

I feel very privileged to have had the experience of being under Sandy's tuition as he introduced me to the beauty, the poetry, the hints and nuances and subtle allusions, and all of the wide range of human emotions — joy, sadness, wonder, nostalgia, concern for friends, humour, sarcasm, etc. — expressed in these songs. In this small collection you will find many succinct verbal portraits of a wide range of Pilbara history, as seen through Ngarla eyes. Clearly there were, among the Ngarla people, men who would have ranked highly in the world of arts and literature — even though they never had the opportunity to become literate.

I fear that even after Sandy has helped me grasp for myself the wit and wisdom, the vibrancy, the poignancy, the zest for life found in many of these songs, my attempts to convey them to other people in English in appropriate poetic ways have often

seemed clumsy in comparison to the skilfully woven threads of the original Ngarla.

My desire has been to present the songs in such a way that thoughtful readers will be able to relive the emotions of the authors when they composed them. If, therefore, you read one of these songs and it leaves you feeling unmoved, unable to enter into the scene for yourself, you can be sure the fault is not with the Ngarla song, but with my failure to express its message well enough to do it justice.

Brian Geytenbeek
Field Linguist, Summer Institute of Linguistics,
Australian Aborigines and Islanders Branch.

Ngarla Country

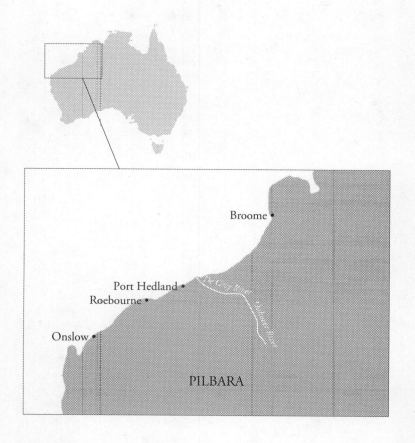

The De Grey River, central to Ngarla country.

Above: Kurtamparanya (Cape Keraudren).
Below: Mikurrnya.

Cultural Introduction

Ngarla country stretched along the coast from Port Hedland eastwards for some 150 kilometres and inland for up to fifty kilometres or more. No accurate count was made, but there were thought to be several hundred Ngarla people in the late 1800s.

Their territory included a wide range of environments. There was the Indian Ocean teeming with fish, the coastline teeming with seabirds, shellfish and crustaceans, and behind the sand dunes there were open grassy plains with rocky outcrops and ranges where emus, kangaroos, wallabies and bilbies abounded. A major river (the De Grey), a minor one (Pardoo Creek) and some tidal inlets lined with mangroves were home to numerous fish and waterbirds — and mosquitoes! Numerous coolabah, cabbage gum and river red gum trees provided hollow nesting sites for corellas by the thousands, as well as possums and native bees, and there are numerous other species of birds throughout Ngarla territory.

Songs in this book mention many of these places and environments in passing, and show an intimate knowledge of the creatures that inhabited them and the weather patterns that influenced them.

The first white settlers along the north-west coast of Australia

arrived in 1863, and within a very few years pastoral leases had been taken up in the areas around Roebourne and the mouth of the De Grey River. Pastoralists would have been unable to establish their leases without considerable help from the Aboriginal people, and they could not have survived for long without Aboriginal seasonal labour. Few white people were ready to face the heat and the hardships of pioneering the harsh Pilbara country, and no convicts were permitted in the northern part of Western Australia. The Aborigines, whose country it was, and who were already well accustomed to the climate, were the logical choice to staff the pastoral ventures.

Before fencing and windmills came onto the scene Aborigines were essential to De Grey River enterprises as shepherds, and their tracking skills and intimate knowledge of their country and its waterholes were of great advantage.

Within a short period of time many had proved themselves capable of handling the practical aspects of pastoral work. Horse breaking and riding, mustering sheep, shearing, scouring wool, loading goods on and off wagons, and transporting them to and from the coastal ships with teams of bullocks or donkeys were all tasks carried out by Ngarla people. They were also involved in the pearling industry, both in dry-shelling (collecting oysters from the reefs as far out as low tides would permit), and as slave labour on pearling luggers.

Meanwhile they carried on their traditional lifestyle much as before. The worst enemies of the Ngarla people were the non-Australian diseases introduced by Europeans and Asians, and against which the Ngarla had no immunity. Many

Above: Makanykarra.
Below: Kantungu (Condon).

Above: Kartiminnya.

Below: Jarrakapujangunya on the De Grey River.

hundreds died in a measles epidemic alone, and many more died of smallpox and respiratory diseases during the early contact years.

By the 1930s, when Alexander Brown was a boy, many of the Aboriginal men on De Grey owned their own horses, and some owned gigs or buggies as well. Several were able to drive motor vehicles. Some managed outcamps. Some knew how to do oxywelding. During World War Two all but five of the staff on the station were Aboriginal, but even before then, many of these skills had found their way into the anecdotal songs.

Types of Ngarla Songs

The Ngarla people had various types of songs. They had no secret/sacred songs themselves, as many Aboriginal groups had, including their inland neighbours, the Nyamal, with whom they shared close relationships, and whose language was closely related to the Ngarla language. If the Nyamal people wished to present a secret corroboree to Ngarla viewers, the Ngarla people would be forewarned, and those not entitled to see the presentation or parts thereof would cover their faces up at the appropriate times.

The only permanent restrictions on Ngarla songs were those applied to *wanarta* initiation songs. These could never be sung by a single person, only by a group, all of whom had themselves been initiated; and *wanarta* songs could only be sung at the appropriate initiation ceremonies. Women did most of the singing at *wanarta* ceremonies.

The *jarlurra* were corroboree songs, that is, they always had a dance attached, a 'choreography'. The *yirraru*, of which sixty-eight are presented in this book, were anecdotal songs. They had no dance attached.

People did not usually set out to compose *jarlurra*. They were not attributed to spirits in the way that secret/sacred Aboriginal songs usually were. The basis for *jarlurra* songs mostly came in dreams and the composer would then fill out the ideas when he woke up. At times a composer's spouse might help with suggestions, and the two would edit the production together. The composer would then ask the group who were with him about putting a *yurnpa* (choreography) to it. The song would then be kept secret, so as not to spoil the fun, until they had worked out the choreography they planned to use with it. They would then premiere it in song and dance form at a public corroboree, arranged for mutual enjoyment and entertainment.

Once a *jarlurra* song had been publicly presented, the song, or brief excerpts from it, could then be sung by anybody, whenever they felt like it. However a full presentation required the dancing as well.

In a full evening's corroboree there might be some twenty different *jarlurra* scheduled, all of which would be sung, in a predetermined order, though not all would be danced. The ones which were only sung were referred to as *kaayi*. They would be fitted in during the intervals while the dancers were resting or preparing for the next dance. Such a *jarlurra* series might take two or three hours or more, allowing for the intervals, and thus provide a whole evening's entertainment. They were always

Above: Jimarlinya (Jijilajangunya, otherwise known as Jijila).
Below: Kurrunya Pool on the De Grey River.

Above: Yurtuputunya (Yurtuputu — name of shells), Cape Keraudren.
Below: Mayawaringunya (on the reef a couple of kilometres off the coast at Condon).

presented at night, by firelight, so that the dancers could assemble 'in the wings' (behind shelters built for the occasion) without the audience being able to see the participants until they danced out into the firelit area.

The *yirraru* did not have nor need any choreography and were composed about specific events or experiences which captured the emotions or fired the imagination, which the composer shared by describing them poetically and musically. He could modify an existing tune to sing his *yirraru* to, or make up a tune of his own.

Unlike *jarlurra, yirraru* were not kept secret until a public presentation could be made — *yirraru* could be sung by anybody, at any time. Some people were gifted at remembering such songs and built up huge repertoires of them, often in several different languages. Alexander Brown is one such person.

If the composer of a *jarlurra* or *yirraru* died, people would refrain from singing that song for some time, out of respect for the deceased, but after a suitable time had elapsed the song could be taken up again.

The sixty-eight songs in this book are all *yirraru*, anecdotal songs composed and sung for pleasure.

Miriny-Mirinymarra Jingkiri

Miriny-Mirinymarra Jingkiri was also known as 'Horse Boy Jimmy', as his work on De Grey Station mainly involved the horses. He spent all his life at De Grey Station usually mustering sheep but once a year mustering cattle for branding. He was also involved with droving — mainly sheep — between De Grey and Port Hedland, a trip which used to take about a week. He was uncle for Wirrkaru Jingkiri. Miriny-Mirinymarra Jingkiri passed away in the late 1930s.

WIRTIYAMARRA

Parta ngaja nyurrala ngani marri,
yankurri, pakarn-pakarnkapu,
paka ngartirringukapu, Wirtiyamarranya.

Parrkuya pirntukarta nyarukarrangura.
Jalyipirnaramalu yirrangka wantanmaraya.

THE UNBEATABLE BLOKE [1]

I'm watching one of you fellows,
an unbeatable bloke, [2]
the one from the rough riverbank area,
the steep bank area,
the man they call Wirtiyamarra.

Parrkuya with her swag [3]
is going off down the riverbed.
At Jalyipirnara up on the cliff
they can share out the winnings.

1 The composer is watching a card game.
2 The cards the man was being dealt always looked good ones.
3 Her roll of money. The unbeatable Wirtiyamarra got beaten — it was Parrkuya who went home with the winnings!

MURRKAMALU JARNTI NYINUYA

Nipuru jarnti ngirnta yarra nyirnti-nyirnti jilkurnmarra
yantaringura,
katalwanti yingkal.

Purtin waya kankarni
para martiri wanyjarntaya.
Wurta-wurta marranymara mangarr marnarra
ngungku jarnta nganyjarranya marayangukunti.

Wuju-wujungurala palu
wampakalya wayi marrinyuru
waya ngunanykarrangurala yulu
kalya yijarrinyuru.

28

THEY BUILT IT RIGHT AT MURRKANYA [1]

Mr Neville [2] put it up,
made out of timber,
sticking up above the surroundings
from down in the hollow,
like it was made for cattle.

Fourteen wires up above,
parallel they put them.
'Always up in the tops of the trees,
they're experts at it.'
He's thought of that,
he knows we're fond of witchetty grubs. [3]

In spite of all that and the parallel wires
we'll still find a way
of continually exchanging little things
through the gaps and cracks.

[1] The Lock Hospital ('Lock-up Hospital') in Port Hedland, built for Aboriginal patients. Within that again was another locked compound in which VD patients were kept.

[2] Mr A O Neville, Chief Protector of Aborigines in WA (1915–1940).

[3] Obviously for people so adept at climbing, the outer man-proof fence with the fourteen rows of barbed wire mentioned in verse 2 (and with the top wires slanted inwards), would be needed to keep them from absconding.

MR NIPURL

Nganungaya kanyiyirnta purlpi pirtila
ngartaly-ngartalyala mulyalkurala murlurnu pirtila.

Kalyangkuya pukuly kuyirnta Kanapantanguru yalya
pukaly-pukalykartaya.
Nganyjarranga Nipurlala milpayanta malya ngarrikura!

Wataku purulu ngaja ngayinykurna
nyarra martikartangurulula.
Yartila ngaya ngalyirla parntu karrikura.

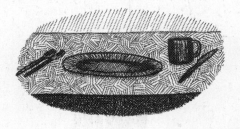

MR NEVILLE

Well fancy that,[1] he's been keeping it for ages for me,
this really old worn-out antique
stuff from way back.

He's been hoarding it, carefully nursing these beaten up
old chattels from Carnarvon.
Neville came here to be a father to us!

Well never mind,[2] I'll down this mouthful.
Later on my neck might recover.

[1] The first verse of this song sets out in masterly sarcasm the composer's reactions to having to use what he regards as very-much second-hand eating gear provided for the inmates of the Lock Hospital in Port Hedland (see song 'Murrkamalu Jarnti Nyinuya', pp 28–29, footnotes 1 and 2).

[2] In verses 2 and 3 he addresses another problem. He knows that the eating gear has been stored ever since the closing down of other Aboriginal VD hostels that had been on Bernier and Dorre Islands, west of Carnarvon. Although he carefully avoids any reference to death or dead people, the thrust of this verse is that these eating utensils have been used by people now dead, and the composer is very concerned about it. In the Aboriginal culture, such things should have been buried with the owner; to use a dead person's belongings was to invite sickness or death. He therefore finds it very difficult to be forced into having to use them. In the end he figures he has no option; his food is on it; the only alternative would be to starve. And maybe this mouthful he is about to swallow will nearly kill him, but hopefully his throat (and he) will recover later.

MURRKANYAKARNI

Yirrkalijikurru marnanyurulu,
nganyjarranga wana jinyji pirnu,
ngupu ngajururr karrimara juraka,
nganyjarranga wii marnanyuru.

Jartangkarla kurrngalala nyayi
nganyjarra Murrkanyakarnirla.
'Palkaya nyayi nganyjarra.
Wanka marnuya, mila ngarrikura?'

'Kulypurr ngani manpiya
pala malukurru-kurru wurrangkura.
Wurta mayararriya pala nganyjarranga
mila ngarriwanti.'

GOING TO THE LOCK HOSPITAL [1]

Making lots of rattling noises,
gobbling up the many miles,
humming a tune,
the truck is carrying us along.

Hey! I didn't realise there were so many of us
going to Murrkanya.
'I wonder how we will fare.
Will we go home better, or
will we go home to die?'

'Memorise, look at those shady red gums.
Their tops will still be swaying in the breeze for us
when we are ready to go home to convalesce.' [2]

[1] See 'Murrkamalu Jarnti Nyinuya', pp 28–29, footnote 1.
[2] Actually here understood as a euphemism for 'die', though there was also the possibility of recovering (Aboriginal patients with various illnesses, not just VD, were sent to the Lock Hospital).

WAYURRKUNTIMALUNGKU

Karlanjarra yiti murru,
mukunta jirntararrangka,
Wayurrkuntimalungku piyarru kanyinmara.

'Mintu! Mintu!' kalyukapu.
Jirtamarra warukarra.
Yirra kanimparrarla,
parnanmarra juntumpi.

Pirlukura pirlukura yartingara purrpi marnu.
Ngapajarrangurarru yilarru, jurtintinyu.

SHIP ANCHORED AT NUMBER 1 WHARF

Bright lights all along it,
a big glow with bright centres of light within it,
keeping Number 1 Wharf illuminated.

'Look lively! Get ready!' Because of the call.
Eyes dazzled.
Heading out the channel northwards,
straight for the open sea.

Waves coming one after another,
he meets them head-on.
Still all brightly lit up,
disappearing into the distance.

A song about a coastal trading vessel leaving the port at night.

KURLINTANYA

Kurlintanya kanyinpiya,
(yulu mungkarra, wirnta pungkurirri),
wanngirrimannyangurarla.
Yulu mingka kayinyu.

Jurta juntu jina man,
para wii marnanyurulurla laanjilu kulpirrikartilu.
Wanakurru Kurlinta!
Kanyin kipangku warlu martaringura.

KOOLINDA *IN HARBOUR*

Look after *Koolinda* there, you fellows,
(huge plucky thing,
all its masts and derricks sticking up),
on account of the cyclone.
It's a plucky thing,
just sheltering there for a while.

He'll head straight out into the wind,
the launch will lead the ship out
as it heads towards the big sea breeze.
Huge *Koolinda!*
The skipper will take care of it
out in the deep water.

The *Koolinda* was a steamer plying the Western Australian coast.

WURRUWANGKANYA JIPAL PIRNU JAWIRILU

Wurruwangkanya jipal pirnu Jawirilu.
Kurnturrjartu wunta murli-murli,
ngayiny parrpa ngarringurulu
yinararra murnaju nyurranga.

Pulangkarti jananmani kanyinpiya winu nyukangkurla.
Waayi nyurranya wungku kurnu Jawirimarralu!

Ngayinykapu pananga — Yirrmarimarrarra
Milkuwarnarra pananga Wawirimarrarra —
Kurri-kurringura yarnangkarla pinurrula
panya warru jarnu.

AT WURRUWANGKANYA JAWIRI IS INCREASING THE COLD

At Wurruwangkanya [1] Jawirimarra is doing
an increase ceremony.
The dust is swirling and eddying,
and his torso is sweating as a result of your
blazing heat.

The ones who increase the heat
are piling on the blankets.
How now? Jawirimarra has got you
huddled in your windbreaks!

The Heat totem belongs to them —
Yirrmari, Milkuwarna, Wawiri [2] —
but in the cold season [3] their fire is dead —
Jawiri has blackened it!

[1] Wurruwangkanya, in Nyamal country, was the increase site for Cold.

[2] Names of three leading men whose totem was Heat, quoted as representatives of all those who had Heat as their totem.

[3] Literally, 'When the Seven Sisters go to rest.' When they set soon after sundown (April to May), the cold season is approaching.

NGANI MARNA KURLINTA KARNUMARRA MIRTA

Ngani marna Kurlinta,
karnumarra mirta,
winta kulyu, ngarrparni,
taparl yinjinkarta.

Karnumarra parrpa kamanpulala!
Ngayiny marrapalu yinjintu
wurla-wurla Mara Pikurrinya.

Wirti ngarringurulu nyurranga wijil murru
marnu.
Kampu-kampu marriya.
Nganil nyurra! Purlpi, wulyulu.

I SAW THE KOOLINDA *IN WHITE PAINT*

I'm looking at the *Koolinda*,[1]
   its whole body white,
with lots of windows, all kinds of them,
   and having two engines.[2]

Warm up your engine!
With homesickness[3] the engine
is churning up the waters of Port Hedland.

In readiness to go he is blowing the whistle
   for you fellows.
They are chivvying each other to hurry up.
You're moving! Right-oh, off you go, westwards.

---

[1] The *Koolinda* was a steamer plying the Western Australian coast.
[2] Although the ship only had one funnel, it had two diesel engines and two propellers.
[3] The *Koolinda's* home port was Perth.

WUPURI

Warru yintirr ngarnu ngurlungka nyinu
witingkalu mali jarnanyurulu
warnmurtalu Wupurinya.

Witamaru waan yartangura wangka
para mali jarnanyurulu,
jantarrmantu yirrarnpi nyininyurulu.

Juntulypirri Marrpawarna.
Kanjipirringura palu,
wakarrilu pangurn marnu.
Wupurilu parrpangka jan.

WUPURI

There's a mob gathered in the house,
with light-hearted laughing and joking about
Wupuri.[1]

Quieter down at the yard
they are still bantering about him in undertones,[2]
well-dressed gentlemen sitting around the rails.

Marrpawarna[3] is sitting perfectly straight.
The horse bucks forwards and sideways
at the same time,
while leaning and turning with him,
with big straight bucks
and with jerking from side to side.
Wupuri will make him sweat.[4]

[1] He was famous as a horse breaker, and they were looking forward to seeing him in action. This song about him is thought to have been composed in the early 1920s.

[2] So as not to frighten the horse, nor distract the rider.

[3] Wupuri's clan name.

[4] Even after the horse has tried every possible trick, and is in a lather of sweat, it will still not have dislodged Wupuri from its back.

WARIYARRANYA NYURRANGA NGURRA PUNGKARRIYA

Purlamilu nyurranga muwarr murru marnu,
yumpukapulu yila jumpintangulu.

Wii marna nyurranya ngarrarti wulyulu.
Kartalu panalu[1]! Yintakapu nyurra Wariyarranya,
nyurranga ngurra pungkarriya.
Wii marna nyurranya ngarrarti wulyulu.

Jampirlirr kartarli ngarrimara pananga[1] juru karriwanti
yaarta nyirnirrkulu yurrumurtu Kuukin.

Martu punyja nyurranya juri pajintaya,
yirlikura wanpari. Kuparu nyurranga.

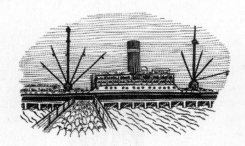

WARIYARRANYA IS NOT YOUR COUNTRY ANY LONGER

Fleming [2] sent a word about you,
  maybe he bribed someone,
  to have you seized and harmed.

He will take you west to Port Hedland [3] forever.
  You poor fellows from Wariyarranya,
  it's not your country any longer.
  He will take you west to Port Hedland forever.

He can open the side of the ship
  ready for you to pour through
into the well-prepared pens in the huge Gorgon.

Your front half is tasty when it is eaten,
  your soup is good.
  You are headed for your graveyard.

---

[1] In these two places the composer switches to the third person pronoun in Ngarla, talking to himself, but in the English translation the second person forms have been retained throughout, to make it easier to follow.

[2] Fleming was a stock and station agent in Port Hedland when this song was composed. The composer suggests that the message is like a magic curse, worked by someone who has been bribed to do it, to have the flock of sheep grabbed and harmed.

[3] Twice in this verse the words 'to Port Hedland' are implied by the direction 'west'. Drovers would take the sheep on foot. On their journey from Wariyarranya, the last camp on De Grey Station was at Karrungu, the government stock-route well on the Ridley River. From there to Port Hedland was a further two- to three-day journey.

Wirrkaru Jingkiri

Wirrkaru Jingkiri's main work was mustering at De Grey Station. When there was no mustering he'd do fencing. In 1946 he joined the strike for pay and better conditions for Aboriginal workers on stations. To earn money he did pearl shelling with the gang at Jijila. He did prospecting around Pilykunykura in the 1950s, and passed away in the 1960s.

WIYURRKARRA

Wurapirri wura ngantayinyu yarlunarra.
Kuntu kaman! Nyinta murti wiyurrkarra.

Yuringi wakarnirnu Pijipangulu.
Warnmurtaya pananya kurnawirtiya!

FAST WORK

He crouches low in the saddle on a fancy horse.
Keep plenty of reserve!

You're working fast and skilfully.
Pijipangu rounded them up and turned them.
Well done! They're all together in one mob!

This song is about Harry Davis riding out and rounding up fresh horses for a muster.

PIYUWIKI

Ngurra martu-martu, waalyanya,
marlparan, Piyuwiki winyja yawilarni.

Yarrka para pirlurru ngani man,
jangku murru marnu,
yarnangkalu jiparnu Ngarlu Jurrkanalu.

BUICK [1]

It's a bumpy road, but the ride's not rough,
it's smooth, let the Buick sway.

He can see a long way ahead,
he let it go free,
he drove in a relaxed [2] manner, that Alec Beeton.

[1] In the first verse the composer is praising the excellent suspension of the Buick, which rides smoothly over the rough road. In the second verse he is praising the skill of the driver.

[2] *Yarnangka* basically means 'leaning against a backrest', but is also used to describe someone who is fully competent, relaxed at his task. He has no need to be tense. He is, in modern parlance, 'laid back'.

KAJIKAYIN NYAYI

Yartingara parrku-parrku marnu,
winta ngarrparni kartarli,
warntaya Karrkarra.

Wurrpangka juntu jiparnu Kajikayin nyayi,
yararta marlirrilu pangkaya jurrkarnu.

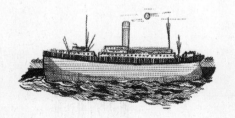

THIS IS THE GASCOYNE [1]

Ploughing through the ocean waves,
many windows in a row, transparent,
skilfully built [2] in Perth.

This *Gascoyne* is going straight up the channel,
flat rudder smoothly parting the water.

[1] The *Gascoyne* was a coastal trading vessel.
[2] Literally, 'timber skilful'. The composer may have been describing the ornate
woodwork in the superstructure, or referring to the shaping of the steel of the hull.
There was, of course, no Ngarla word for steel, but the use of the complimentary suffix
–ya ('well done!') shows that he is admiring the skilful processing and shaping involved
in the construction of the ship. In later years processed metals came to be described as
'stone' rather than 'timber'.

MIRTANYA

Ngantu nganya juntu marnu palu mirtanya nganu?
Paja yila nyayi.

Ngurtu-ngurtu ngani manpiya,
ngamarrangka warlakakarrijangu.

Murnajula nyini ngajapa tukurrampilu.
Wayi ngaja nyina mirlkaya pungarnu?

THE OLD ROOSTER

Who told the old fellow [1] about me?
I think he's cross about me.

Look at him stamping,
holding that spear poised.

In response now stay still for me with my club. [2]
How does it feel after I hit you on the head?

[1] This song is about an old and cheeky rooster, being described as an angry warrior.
[2] This refers to the old cultural fighting rules, which required the combatants to take turn and turn about with their blows.

MAPARNKARRA

Miru-miru nyinila. Wanyja?
Waayi milpayan maparnkarra?
Nyayi parnunga tayimu.

'Layinapu yirra nyiniya!'
Jirli yajirnu, jaamanyjakarra.
'Jirlikurnu! Yarra!'

DOCTOR'S DAY [1]

Let's all wait anxiously. (What else can we do?)
What's happening? Is the doctor coming?
It's time for him.

'Get in a line!' He stabbed the arm, it's numb.
'Fold up your arm! [2] Off you go!'

---

[1] At the Lock Hospital.

[2] To hold the cotton swab in place until the spot stopped bleeding.

WANYJAKARNI

Wanyjakarni pirntu murrijangu?
Ngunyikarni nganarna puurnmarrikura!

Kurlurlu jurangarra nyurranga yartangura.
Yaarta kartirirrilu nyurranya.
Wayi wakurr jarnu!

WHERE ARE YOU GOING?

Where are you fellows going with all that stuff?
We're going to that yard to holler and yell! [1]

The dust is billowing up for you in the yard.
You're all fenced in in that yard. [2]
See if that'll hold the lot of you!

---

[1] They were heading for a day's work in the sheep yards.
[2] Both sheep and people!

Yintilypirna Kaalyamarra

Yintilypirna Kaalyamarra was also known as 'Shaw River Smiler'. He did mostly mustering with sheep on Shaw River Station. This station was actually a big outcamp for De Grey Station. He was also an artist and his black ink line drawings can be found at Dalgety House in Port Hedland. When in Port Hedland he used go sailing on Jimmy Monaghan's yacht with Jimmy's son Tommy. He passed away in the early 1940s.

MARRPAWARNA

Parta marra pirnu Wupurlan Marrpawarnalu,
yinjinpa jarnarra muurrkarra piturulkapurla,
murti kanyjilipa yara nguntuntu karri.

THE OVERLAND

Marrpawarna [1] accelerated the Overland, [2]
engine thrusting forwards
with a throaty noise as a result of the petrol,
swooping round the bends
with a whining roar.

[1] The same man as featured in the song 'Wupuri'.
[2] A brand of vehicle used on the station.

KANA WARUKAYINYJANGURA

Kurturtulu ngaja yirtikurla partu marrangka
yilpirtirri [2] yarnangka nyinu,
walkurtarri [2] jarna japarr ngan.

Walu purturrungura, yirtinykarra,
pirrpangka kanyin,
walkurtarri purnura [2] nyinu murtirnarra [2]
yarna japarr ngan.

Kana warukayinyjangura nyurrala wilyila parrakura
kamarnu,
warangarripuru, wakartarri, Parrarurrumarra.

IN THE GLOW OF EARLY DAWN [1]

I'm part way along as you fly overhead
on your journey,
your instruments [2] all in a line,
backing you up, [3]
your instruments [2] flashing behind you.

On your magic cord,
connected together in sequence,
you are keeping them bright.
Your tools of trade [2] that give you your
authority [3] are flashing.

With the increasing glow of the dawn
I can see you faintly,
like a wind from the west, thinly veiled,
turning, [4] Parrarurrumarra.

[1] This song is about glimpsing a sorcerer flying high overhead at early dawn, on
some mission of harm to someone.

[2] These four words refer to four different items in the sorcerer's tools of trade. What
they were made of and what their specific uses were have not been identified.

[3] These instruments were an essential part of the sorcerer's spiritual authority.
Without them he would not have been able to carry out his mission.

[4] The word 'turning' here refers to a changing of direction, a curving onto a new
course, not to a rotating movement.

PURARRKA

Murrurlungura murta pimpurrkurnu,
murru mantangu, ngupu ngajururr kayinyjangu.
Kayila para ngurra yarrkarra!

Nyirturalu kanji yirra wirti
maarnu ngurra yalalunya.
Purnumpurnungu murru warnpa!
Purarrka nganu!

DRIVING TO PURARRKA [1]

Motor accelerating through the stony ridges,
set free, singing a tune.
Take us to faraway country!

The mirage is lifting the hillside cliffs up and down in
rising undulating country. [2]
Now we're coming towards massive hills
and rocky outcrops!
That's how Purarrka looks to me!

[1] This is the name of a prominent hill out towards the Great Sandy Desert.

[2] The composer is describing his progressive approach towards the far-distant hill, shimmering in the mirage. *Yalalunya* is the name for the undulating but gradually rising beginnings of the foothill country when nearing a range.

PALKAYA NGALI PALU WARNTA PIYAN-PIYANTA

Palkaya ngali palu warnta piyan-piyanta.
Ngayinyala ngali warlu puruyinyu!
Kujungurru piparuluya ngalinya
ngumpa kutuljapanmara.

Jiyipu palkarta karra mantangura
nyintapa ngurntirri karri.
Jiyipu palkarta karra mantangura
nyintapa pulyurrukapu.

Minjil ngarntumarra wara
ngunta-nguntayinyu ngalinga,
minjil ngarntumarra puumungura yarnaka.

Yilyipirri-yilyipirriluya ngalinga
tingkila ngaalani jiparnu.
Yartingara martunjurr-martunjurrya
ngali partangka ngaalininyu!

I WONDER HOW ROUGH IT IS GOING TO BE FOR US

I wonder what sort of ride we'll get,
with the boat jerking around like this.
Our feelings are a bit fearful! [1]
The vastness of the ocean will put us
out of sight of land.

While you are holding the jib tightly
it vibrates noisily in the wind.
While you are holding the jib tightly
the spray rattles against it.

The huge cloth mainsail is flapping for us,
the huge cloth mainsail attached to the boom.

The small waves cause
the boat to rock for us.
In the bigger rougher waves
we rock in a different way!

[1] The two men are not, in fact, worried about their safety, but they're pretty sure
that they are in for a rough trip in the choppy seas.

YIRRA, KUJI, YIRRA, KARTI NGAYIRRMANI

Yirra, kuji, yirra, karti ngayirrmani.
Purntura ngarra maninyu.
Kapalya kurru marnanyurulu
ngurra parlangkarna-parlangkarna kamarnu.

Ngurntika wangka yulayinyu.
Ngurra kunti marnu ngurlungkangulu.
Parlkarranguraya kuji muurrkarra, jinyjirrarangka.

Ngarri para pungarnu,
kurlurlu karti ngampurrjarli marnu ngurntijartulu.
Jamukarra! Warlpa warninyu.
Karnkulypangungu.

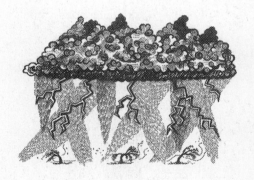

ROWS AND ROWS OF RAIN CLOUDS

Cloudbank, rain, cloudbank,
row upon row of them.
The big upper-layer clouds are rising.
As a result of the host of little clouds
multiplying the country is heating up.

In the constant thunder it talks,
telling us it's coming.
The downpour is drenching the countryside.
In the open country the raindrops are causing a soft
roaring sound,
as the swathe of the downpour passes.

Lightning is striking at the front,
the storm is causing the dust to swirl around.
Sudden silence! Splashing of falling raindrops.
Karnkulypangu was the cause of this! [1]

[1] Rain was Karnkulypangu's *kalyartu* (totem); he was therefore in charge of its increase, and so is considered to be the one responsible for this downpour.

PANGANYJALU KARRI YILPIWARNA

Ngurra martu-martu waalyanyakurla!
Jurtarinypa murru marnu kunmungkalu,
muurta marnta ngurrpungka jirntararrangka.

Ngurntirri jari-jari, murru man ngurra yarrkawanti,
yinjinpa ngunanykarra,
karla jirntararrangkalula waranpa ngurra pirrparnu.

Yirlku parrakarta, marlparan yawilarninyu,
kurlurlu winyja mukulirti, kankara purlkayinyu.

Yarnangkalu karri ngurra parranywanti,
murti yirrarlirli Piyuwiki.
Kiya para kiya panganyjalu karri Yilpiwarna.

Kanji wungkurruralu jurta murlinykunu,
ngurra yintiri jarnu.
Kunmungka jirntalyarrangka kayila,
laampu pilalykarra pintangu.

72

ARTHUR IS DRIVING IT CAREFULLY

No need to worry about the bumpy road!
Let her go like the wind in the twilight,
with the motor purring and the headlights on.

Roaring along effortlessly,
let her go ready for far distant country,
engine working perfectly,
the bright lights lighting up the whole countryside.

Wheels spinning fast, car rocking along smoothly,
dust trailing out behind, billowing upwards.

In a relaxed way he is taking it for a long trip,
the pebbles rattling up underneath the
Buick's mudguards as it travels.
Arthur is changing the gears carefully.

The speeding is stirring up the wind alongside,
the country flashes past.
Let's take it in the headlights in the twilight,
the scenery ahead flashing in the lamplight.[1]

---

[1] Referring to the way the scenery is lit up as the car crests a rise, and then disappears
as the headlights point down into the next hollow.

NGURRA PARTA NGAYINYU NGAJAPA WANGKURRUNGURA
KAPUNGURALA

Yirra wirli-wirli,
kanji mungkarra kanji jaruntarri-jaruntarrimara.
Papa warrungura minjilpa jangku para.

Jurnti ngarurr pirnkurrpa Karlkajarranya
ngurra yumpa mirtarri.
Jurnti ngarurrpa Karlkajarranya jinarralu wanyjanpila.

Ngurra parta ngayinyu ngajapa
wangkurrungura kapungurala.
Ngunyi yila panyja wirtingarra pala
payinta Walal-Mulyanya.

Jurta yanganpila mulya yijungku
ngarlinymarra kanji ngurrpungkalula.
Yilyirri pangka jurrkarnu,
yartingara jananmani-jananmanikapu
warnta yangka-yangkayinyu.

Jiipu jirti ngungku karra marna kanji-kanjinyjangu.
Miin jirtila nyirr marnu purlakangura yirtinykarra.

Wira purrintangurala palkarta yakula palu,
mulya mungkarralula yali wangkurru jurrkarnu.

74

THE COASTLINE LOOKS STRANGE TO ME FROM OUT HERE

The bow wave is rippling,
the long sides of the boat rock slowly from side to side.
Out on the deep water I'm easing the mainsail.

There is the long stretch of curved inlets
and sandy white beaches at Karlkajarranya.
With a beeline we'll bypass those inlets of Karlkajarranya.

It looks like a different country to me from out on the open sea.
Maybe that really high sand dune is Walal-Mulyanya Point.

We'll follow the wind, with the bow pointing east,
as the boat heels perfectly to match the change of course.
We cut the spray and turn it to tiny droplets,
the timber of the boat shakes
from the successive pounding of the waves.

He is holding the jibsheet firmly
while the boat is being jerked from side to side.[1]
The mainsheet rope rattles through the sheaves
of the blocks linked together in series.

The wind strains to pull the boat offcourse,
but I'm holding the rope firmly and confidently,
the long bow rushing over the deep open sea.

---

[1] The boat is now cutting through the waves diagonally, and each wave tries to thrust
the bow of the boat a bit to one side.

WIRNTA KATAKA PUNGKURIRRI, PURNAKUJARRA

Wirnta jayin pirnu wangkurrungura,
wirnta kataka pungkurirri,
purnakujarra.

Jirtamarra pananga nyinila.
Mirlungkurniny mayinyjangurra, paarlanku,
kulpirri karti ngarntumarra, wara ngalparra.

JAPANESE PEARLING FLEET [1]

Masts partly hidden on the open sea,
now the whole boat visible,
next only the tops of the rigging in view.[2]

Keep your eye out for them.
They are gathering again, for pearling,
sails in the sea breeze,
scattered across the horizon.

[1] This song was composed before World War Two.
[2] This verse refers to the way the boats alternately rose into sight as they crested the big waves and then sank down into the troughs in between.

WIYANU NGAYA MANGKURU WAJARRI

Ngarrungkanguru minga-minga.
Yurlu karrimara marntipukarra, jampirr mirta!
Yurnungka ngaja warringanarra.

Yirrji palu, kuminy wanyjarna, nyarra partanyal,
pawurta wurntu murru marnu, yurlari purlkayinyu.

Jinyjirr ngara-ngarakartalu pirlurru.
Wilypa purrirnu,
yarangarra purlpa wariny marnu,
warlany warninyu.

SHOOTING A KANGAROO

Waking up from sleep uneasy.
Let the old boomer, white stripe,[1] stay in his camp!
I'm an expert with red kangaroos.

Aiming at him, putting the gun right on target,
one barrel, powder all gone, smoke billowing.

Blood spurting leaving a trail along the track.
He's pulled off balance,
red kangaroo's tail flipped,[2]
he toppled and fell.

[1] Only the male red kangaroos have this white blaze from the sides of their jaws down their chests to their groins.
[2] Flipped: literally 'in another direction'. This is the last thing you see when the roo finally topples.

NYIRTURALU

Nyirturalu ngurra ngajapa nyanta maarnu.
Karti wulyulu, yarrka, pantayanya.
Jurtintinyu Karukarti.

Yapurru kana-kana marna ngurra mirtarri.
Pararra kana-kana marna karti yiju Jaangarra.

Jarturtu wuntumarra purnulyurr,
kata pukarn kayinyu,
nyirnti-nyirnti warnta kurnari
Punyjurnmarranya.

THE MIRAGE DID IT

The mirage is bringing the country close for me.
I'm heading west,[1] it's a long way, not close.
It feels as if Karukarti is getting further away.

Now glancing north, the country is limestoney.
Later, glancing across the open plain,
Jaangarra is eastwards.

The gum tree crowns are a mass of dense foliage,
a forest you can see from afar,
many clumps of timber all together at
Punyjurnmarranya.

---

[1] The phrase *karti wulyulu* is literally 'lap west'. It means that the person is facing westwards at the time. In this particular song the composer is doing a mill-run on horseback, on Shaw River Station. He refers to different places as seen from different angles as he travels across the countryside.

JARRURRUPURU

Piruwarra kanarakarti, jukany wakarnin,
yirnti jarnti nyirnu.
Purarramalu marlu warninyu.

Purrungungura nyanta karliny yijila.
Winyja wira karla marnu.
Palkaya nyinta nganya pirlurr wakarnin.
Ngayiny nganyju-nganyju jarrurrupuru.

Ngananyayi juntu kankara wurangkarna wurtarriyan,
yirtalirri purnura nyinu walupurturru yirtinykarra?

COMPLETELY WEAKENED

Ascending towards the light, turning it neatly,
he thrusts his stick [1] upright into the ground.
A moving shadow falls at Purarra.

Flying he returns here from the east.
Something long is waving effortlessly.
I am wondering if you will turn my spirit round.
I am feeling breathless and completely weakened.

Who is that standing bending over me,
with your medical instruments all in a line? [2]

[1] Normally *yirnti* means a walking-stick, but in this case the stick is shorter, one of the medicine man's instruments.

[2] The medicine man would have had several small instruments for different purposes. Here they are all in a line, tucked into his hair belt.

MARLAJI KANYINPILA

Ngunyingkajarra, jamantamanta, mala-malaninyu,
ngunyingka kalya pungarnu,
mujura jarra-jarra marnu.

Ngarru nyinila para ngurntikakapurra,
wartangan, jamantamanta kankarni,
purtungka yirra japarr ngarnu.

Yintarra kanyinpila ngurra mapany-mapany jantangu,
jinyjirr yanirnanyurulu japarnu
parlparr warrukurla.

Marlaji kanyinpila palanya kaarr warninyjangu,
marlaji kanyinpila mayangka muurrkarrakapu.

STEADY SPRING RAIN

Here, there, and everywhere, rapid flashing,
storm staying in the one place,
still striking, scattering the clouds.

Relax about the noise, friends,
the thunder, the flashing now overhead,
the front of the storm all lit up.

It will rain all night and make the country
soaking wet, a broad swathe of pouring
rain hiding the night sky.

This spring rain will fall steadily,
at times a soft swishing sound,
at times loudly drumming on the roof.

YILILINGURRPAMALU WARLPA PILYURL MARNU JARAMARRA

Wangkurru karti wakanirnu puyinykartulu,
karnapuka jarnti-jarntiyinyu Kanyintingurrpamalu.

Kuluwa manta-mantayinyu.
Karti jamanta yurlarirri ngarlu ngalparra,
karti yulu-yulu.
Kuji nyirntukarra, jipal pintangu.

Jarrawaringura jamantamanta, yirrkaliji.
Karti yampuka.
Yililingurrpamalu warlpa pilyurl marnu jaramarra.

RAINDROPS SPLASHING INTO DEEP WATER AT TURTLE ISLAND

The light showers are following the horizon
out over the open sea,
the tops of the cumulus clouds are
sticking up at Little Turtle Island.

Now broad rain is hanging around.
Constant lightning inside the approaching
length of cloud, coming determinedly.
Vigorous downpour,
started by the rainmaker.

All lit up, lightning flickering,
rattling thunder diminishing.
Storm past, noise fading into the distance.
At North Turtle Island raindrops are splashing
into the deep water.

Wapirrku Kanturrpamarra

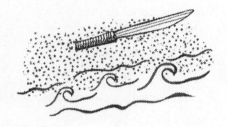

Wapirrku Kanturrpamarra worked at the slaughter yard near Pretty Pool in Port Hedland. He passed away in the early 1920s.

PUPUPUKARRA

Wanangkangu murti-murtiyinyu,
jarlurayinyu,
pupupukarra!

Wanyjarra ngaya para wurrurra wakarnilu?
Ngunparrngari-ngunparrngari,
nyirnti-nyirntiyima yangkurrwartarnu!

DUST STORM

Whirlwinds darting about,
dust stretching out,
wind rushing and roaring!

Which shelter should I turn to?
Groping and stumbling,
groping and stumbling
(through the wind, blinded by the dust),
flying objects hitting all around me!

WILANGKU

Wilangku ngani marna wurrurru yunpa
wakartarri wakartarri Jarrartangura.

Nganungala yirraru yinmawanti.
Pukurrkura nyurra ngukurrungu,
wirnta marntarnu wirnta-wirntangu.

Jurrka ngani manpiya pananya ngurtu-ngurtu,
pikunkurla-pikunkurla Jangarimarranya!

KIMBERLEY PEOPLE

I'm watching the Kimberley people circling [1]
in the style of the Jarrarta [2] Dance.

(This is my song for dancing later!) [3]
You're decorated all over, your headgear
is fastened on,
sticking up from the back of your head. [4]

Look at them dance, a rapid-stamp dance, [5]
Look at Jangari in action, zigzagging! [6]

[1] This reduplicated (and therefore lessened or distributive form) of 'circling' refers not to moving around in complete circles, but to dancing back and forth in curving lines, twisting and turning, in contrast to dancing in straight lines.

[2] *Jarrarta* is not the name of a style of dance, but the name of the particular corroboree that the Kimberley dance reminds him of.

[3] A cheeky 'aside' built into the song by the singer. He was composing a song about a dance; maybe later someone else would do a dance to his song!

[4] *Wirnta-wirntangu* refers to decorated sticks projecting upwards from the back of the head, held in place with a *yakirr* (headband). The bark was first removed from the sticks, and then short lengths of the outer layers of wood were peeled back down the length of the sticks, but not removed. The resultant thin shavings curled into little rolls.

[5] *Ngurtu-ngurtu* is a dance style involving a rapid stamping of the feet, like running on the spot, but stamping while doing so.

[6] *Pikunkurla-pikunkurla* refers to ducking and dodging around obstacles, but in the context of a dance it is a measured progression across a cleared space.

MANGARRJARRA PARLKARRAKAPUMALU

Pipu-pipu, kurlartarra-kurlartarra,
Parlkarrakapumalu kurnturr kanyin kumurumuru.

Jirirrkapumalu jinany-jinany karri,
pakarr pala yara wangka karri, purrpurrkura.

AEROPLANE AT THE RACE-COURSE [1]

Engine idling, revving up,
at Parlkarrakapunya[2] it is kicking up the dust
just before sunrise.

At Jirirrkapunya[3] it is bouncing,
up in the air it is roaring, fully equipped.[4]

[1] This was the first aeroplane to visit Port Hedland. It is pictured warming up and taking off from what is now the Port Hedland Oval.

[2] Parlkarrakapunya (plain-having-place) was the name of the flat strip of ground that stretches from where the Esplanade Hotel now stands right round past Puriyakannya (the Native Well, now marked as part of the Heritage Trail) to the Four Mile Creek. From the east of the Oval a limestone ridge lies along its northern edge.

[3] Jirirrkapunya (prickles-having-place) lay to the north of Parlkarrakapunya, on the other side of the limestone ridge, along where McGregor Street now runs. It was named after the very spiny species of spinifex, *Triodia secunda*, that grew there.

[4] Purrpurrkura referred to someone or something fully prepared for its role, such as a dancer in full regalia.

KARNURURRUMARRA

Marla jiya-jiya, ngakamarnarra.
Jirirrkalu ngurra japarnu.
Malparumarra.

Yankurri ngani marna wirangu pungantangu,
jarlka julu-julu, yirra jarnangka.
Juparumarranya.

Yapurrupurrularri marrkurungurakarta,
ngananykura-ngananykura.
Warilpa kanyirri Wirrkarumarralu.

Malyarnu wilya-wilyayinyu, kuna murntu jarnanyuru!
Miriny-mirinymarra jarlka waarnupulala,
yinyjari-yinyjaringuralu.

Ngalangka nguntily marnu,
karnu puyumarra, marlkarrimanu.
Paparumarra.

Ngalangka nganyjarimpirrkurla jirntiyarrangura.
Warlu marri, ngayirrkajarra karri.
Karnururrumarra.

HAMMERHEAD

He's a stranger bringer,[1] an expert
at carrying messages.[2]
Northern wobbegong sharks are covering the whole area.[3]
That's Malparumarra.[4]

I'm watching him thrashing around at top speed,[5]
fins in a line, rows and rows of teeth.
That's Bluntnose Sixgill Shark.

He's got it in his teeth, mincing it up,
shreds going everywhere.[6]
Bignose Shark has split open a carcass.

He chewed it slowly, guts too, the whole lot!
Bull Shark is showing his fins,[7]
and eating with enjoyment.

Here there's a mighty surge,[8]
enormous body, capable of killing.
That's Tiger Shark.

Here we have eddies of sand in the area.
He starts suddenly, causing two bands full width.[9]
That's Hammerhead.

[1] *Marla jiya-jiya*, translated here as 'stranger bringer', is an idiomatic expression. By itself *jiya* means 'itchy nose'. If your nose is itchy, it is often said that a stranger is coming to see you. In this verse the expression is used because when this little shark appears it won't be long before 'strangers' (his mates, and all the bigger species of sharks) will arrive too.

[2] The feeling is not that the northern wobbegong shark sends messages, but that each time he swims off and then comes back again for another mouthful, other sharks will come with him, almost as if he had gone to fetch them.

[3] The setting of this song is Pretty Pool, a tidal inlet some eight kilometres east of Port Hedland, where the slaughterhouse used to be. The offal and any carcasses that had gone bad were thrown into the creek. It didn't take long for large numbers of sharks to gather whenever slaughtering was in progress.

[4] All six men named in the six verses of this song were members of the Jingkiri clan. They are named in order from youngest/smallest (Malparumarra) through to oldest/biggest (Karnururrumarra), to match the relative average sizes (as seen close in to the shore) of six species of sharks.

Relationships were as follows:

> Malparumarra, likened to a *jirirrka* (verse 1) was the youngest son of Miriny-Mirinymarra (verse 4).
>
> Juparumarra (verse 2) was another of Miriny-Mirinymarra's sons.
>
> Wirrkarumarra (verse 3) was a son of Karnururrumarra (verse 6).
>
> Miriny-Mirinymarra (verse 4), Paparumarra (verse 5) and Karnururrumarra (verse 6) were the three oldest brothers in their family, quoted in ascending order of age.
>
> *jirirrka* = northern wobbegong shark
>
> *juparurru* = bluntnose sixgill shark
>
> *wirrkarurru* = bignose shark
>
> *miriny-miriny* probably = bull shark (an appropriate size, and frequently found in rivers and estuaries)
>
> *paparurru* = tiger shark
>
> *karnururru* = hammerhead shark.

[5] The bluntnose sixgill shark is not a thresher shark, but it twists and turns vigorously in a frenzy of feeding.

[6] The bignose shark lunges towards a carcass, taking a huge bite out of it as he strikes, then ploughs straight on. As he chews on his mouthful, shreds are scattered outwards.

[7] Literally, 'gives his fins'; the tips of his fins show briefly above the surface.

[8] Not a splash, such as when it breaks the surface, but a violent underwater swirl as the tiger shark enters the melee.

[9] Swimming close to the bottom, when a hammerhead shark suddenly accelerates towards his prey, eddies of fine sand billow up on either side of his wide head and leave a double trail behind him, highlighting his presence.

YAMPARNA

Yamparna karta
pangkayinyu wurla-wurlangura,
yilyirrikarti ngayirrmani, ngapurlarnu!

Kartarrapuka waril nguntuntu
ngananykura-ngananykura!

MANTA RAYS AND HUMPBACKS

Manta rays come up into sight
in the turbulent water,
lines of spray, upheaval!

Humpback whales breaching
and splashing thunderously
here, there and everywhere!

This is a very old song, composed before Sandy was born.

WAKARLANGARTIMALU

Purrmartuya panalu kalyu jirumarra,
wayi marrinyuru, Wakarlangartimalu.

Jurirrkapumalu wurru warni maraya.
Pikurrinya ngurra ngakarnu laki-lakilu.

AT NELSON POINT [1]

They are doing lots of high-pitched yelling,
asking one another questions, at Nelson Point.

Right at Jurirrkapu [2] there are big mobs landing.
Asians are crowding Hedland harbour.

[1] A song about Asian fishermen arriving in the harbour.
[2] Jurirrkapunya covers the area from Hunt Point right round to Harriet Point, about where the mouth of the Hammersley Boodari Iron tunnel is.

JIRRIRTINMALU

Kupalyayanyangku kanyinpila pananya,
purrulayinyjangu Jirrirtinmalu,
kuta mirntiny mayinyjangu!

Wurrpa-wurrpangura winyja, jurukarrimaraya,
ngurntirri-ngurntirringura.
Kumpana nyinimara, puwa yarntartarra
ngarlukurnanyuru.

AT JIRRIRTINNYA

Without any sleep we were holding them,
lots of lowing[1] right at Jirrirtin,
lots of clicking of horns!

They're moving in the loading race, let 'em go,
with a hollow echoing noise.
Let the *Koombana*[2] stay there,
for four hundred (pouring) one after another into its hold.

[1] The word refers to a lot of creatures all making their individual noises at the one time, such as flies buzzing, a crowd talking, or in this case cattle lowing.

[2] Since the *Koombana*, a coastal steamship, was only three years old when it sank in 1912, this song must have been composed between 1909 and 1912.

Katakapu

Katakapu did mustering stockwork of cattle and sheep on De Grey Station. He also did the cooking in the mustering camp. His wife, Dolly Pananykarra (cousin of Waparla Pananykarra), was the main cook. Dolly baked the bread for the station staff. Katakapu drove the horsedrawn spring-cart. This cart would carry enough food, swags and equipment for ten to twelve musterers. Katakapu joined the 1946 strike and subsequently joined the Nomads on Strelley Station. He went back to De Grey Station in the 1960s when conditions had improved for Aboriginal workers.

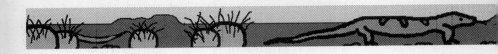

PAMPANULU JINA MARNA NGURRA PANALALA

Pampanulu jina marna ngurra panalala.
Karlka-karlka mirnilypurru
yururtu ngalanya ngayiny kanyilkunti.

Murrulu ngurra yartara —
ngayinyja ngurra wara-wara.
Jalkukurru pukarnkarri warnta
jilukarra Marlanyjinya yinta.

A STRANGER TO THIS COUNTRY, I'M FOLLOWING THEM

I'm a stranger to this country,
so I'm tracking along with these others.
I like this area, with its many beautiful[1] gullies.

Extensive rocky hilly country —
I'm feeling a bit lost in this country.
Lots of cadjebut canopies[2]
in line at Marlanyjinya waterhole.

[1] The word is used of highly decorated dancers in a corroboree.
[2] They are beyond a rise, so he can't see the bases of the trees yet.

PARTA MURRI KARNARANTU YARRKA WANYJARRI

Parta murri karnarantu yarrka wanyjarri,
wirlarra kankara, ngungku wirli marri,
kaniyilu nyaarr kanimparralu.

Kunmukarti jampa yakula pananyja wurtarrikura.
Warru warnngatarrinyurulu mankura.
Yingirr kanyinpila pintiringura!

110

DRY-SHELLING

The really big tide is going out a long way,
the moon is above, holding it just right.
The low tide out northwards is making a soft sound.

As soon as it's light enough let's go
out and stand on the reef.
A dark mass is moving back and forth
lifting the rocks.[1]
Keep on moving over the shallow reef!

[1] Referring to the dark mass of people moving around on the reef. They were lifting the loose rocks, looking for the pearl-shell oysters underneath.

MARRAPA PILURURRUNGU WANGKURRURRA JUNTU

Kanyinpila ngalanya jirlparra, mulya wirtingarra,
marrapa pilururrungu wangkurrurra juntu.

Wara ngarntujilu tingki mulya
kanimparra wirnpirri jiparnu,
partangka juntu maru kayinyjangura.
Ngumpa yila nyurra!

Yartingara ngani marna parta yirra panyjarukarra.
Pajartulu tingkila paarl pungan,
munal yata jarnu.

Ngarlinymarra liyu wakanin kanji wula panta yaanu.
Jaayapangungu.
Jirrparnpa warnta kurlarta pajartu yarrurra.

EAGER TO HEAD FOR THE OPEN SEA

We've got this fancy yacht here, nose in the air,
ready to head straight for the open sea.

The huge sail causes the nose of the boat
to dive down,
on another wave it is made to rear up.
You're out of sight![1]

I'm looking across the top of
the huge mounded waves.
The big waves thump the boat,
pushing it in the opposite direction.[2]

Whenever the boat heels as it turns,
the gunwale goes close to the water.
Jimmy Monaghan is the man involved.
This timber boat is well built,
well able to cope with the big waves.

[1] The boat has plunged down into a trough.
[2] The forward motion of the boat is checked by each wave as it hits.

JANKURNA YANGARRIYA

'Ngunyi yila kartanungu
jankurna purntu warninyuru.
Miru yanya, kupapirri yampirn yananyjangu,
yarrka piyanya ngani marnu,' Pukarrpamarralu.

Panta ngani marnangurulu nyumpalanga,
murrilyi witi yangka marnu, pikun-pikuntu.
Yila nyumpalanya nyayingku minta wanyjanpula.

Pajanpin piyanga murti jangkungarrarra,
Yirrmarimarralu, ngampikuluya
nyinu piyalu yalkirrira nyurtarninykarra.

Juntu ngani marnu marlurrara Kulparrimarralu,
yirtiwarra mulya yiju pirlurru,
winyja, murru marnu.

Warritalu Wawirimarralurla kartingka yarrkapirti,
nyinta wayi wakurr jarnu.
Nyantiya pangkarlangkarla pii puninyala yinyal
murru marnu.

EMU CHASE

'I think that's an emu way over there,
with his breast feathers bobbing up and down.
I'm not just imagining it, he's going head down,
a long way off, I can see his neck silhouetted.
I saw two of them faraway,' said Jack.[1]

After seeing you two from close up,
he shook his tail feathers playfully at you,[2]
dodging from side to side.
Perhaps these two emus will leave you behind.[3]

Speed up for those two running so easily, Teddy,
side by side, frightened of you,
those twin male emus, together.

He saw the one he wanted, prime emu, Harry did. Fast
chase, nose heading east now, on course,[4]
let him go, give up chasing now.

The final man,[5] Henry, welcomed him
into his lap from a long way away.
Well, you've as good as got him now,
that horse with a big white blaze on his forehead,
that grey pony, you gave him full rein.[6]

[1] Jack is skiting a bit here about his superb eyesight!

[2] 'Shook his tail feathers' indicates 'beginning to run'.

[3] Literally, 'leave your nose behind'.

[4] The hunters had previously chosen one of their number to deliver the coup de grace, the mortal wound, and had been steering the emus in his direction.

[5] The *warrita*, the one chosen to finish the emu off.

[6] That is, allowed the pony to gallop 'flat out', and thus got into a position such that the final kill was assured.

NGANANYAKARRA NGANYJARRA NGANIL NGARRI

Yintiri wakarnirnu, ngayinyju marrapalu.
'Warnta karlu-karlu palarr kajunjarra
luwutu warnikatangka!'

'Ngananyakarra nganil ngarri nganyjarra?
Mapalyanyangka?'
'Japajarra nganil jinarra wirlarrakarti.'

Parta marra pirnu ngurra
parlkarrakarrangura Kurrkarakarni.
Nguya-nguya, ngungku pakurta,
yinjinpa pirlurruyanya.

Yinyal murru marnu yirri kanimparra,
kurntarriyanya purijirra para,
partangka nyaarr marnu yilku murrulungura.

Jintararrangka Piyayiti jawarrany murtipa jajukarra,
jungkurl pirnu karti wurruru ngurrarra
marliny karturra.

Yintin marramarralu kayinyu ngurra yumpa-yumparra,
Yamarlingurrpamalu jinanyku,
taya nyangkaly manmara.

Jurnti ngarrparnilu ngurntirri pumarr punganmara
Yarnajangulu. Ritiyayita yukuntarri!
Yartujangumalu jampa wurtarri.

Mirnarrangura karti wurruru Yirrka-Pukarangura
pirrjarta jangkarri jungkurl pirnu.
Nganta-Ngantangura yinjinpa karta
nyangkarr manmara.

NIGHT DRIVE IN A V-8 BUCKBOARD

Darting here and there,[1] eager to get going.
'Let's tie the load tightly on the buckboard!'[2]

'When will we be on the move?
After sunset?'
'After supper we'll move, nonstop in the moonlight.'

He's really speeding across the
plains country to Kurrkara.[3]
The engine is rough, not too good,
not running smoothly yet.

He really let it go down the steep slope,
with no fear of the bridge.
The wheels make a different sort of noise
on the stony patches.

In the dazzling beam the V-8 is running
really fast now,
speeding southwards through the darkness
towards the open country.

Concentrating in the sandy country,
skimming along past Yamarlingurrpa.
Let the tyres hum.[4]

The many bends at Yarnajangu
are bouncing back the engine's booming roar.
Steam, radiator!
At Yartujangu he is standing for a while.

In the pool of light heading south at Yirrka-Pukara
the vehicle is speeding fast.
At Nganta-Nganta the engine's exhaust
is throbbing perfectly.

---

[1] *Yintiri wakarnirnu* means 'going here, there and everywhere'. The driver, Billy Hill, manager of De Grey Station, is constantly changing direction as he goes to various buildings (store, stables, windmill room, etc.) on the station, collecting all the things he has to take out to the outstation.

[2] *Warnta karlu-karlu* (literally 'timber lightweight') refers to the buckboard, which in those days had timber tray and sides.

[3] Kurrkara was the name of the place where the old Broome Highway crossed the De Grey River on a bridge, about a mile south of the De Grey homestead.

[4] The word for this noise is difficult to translate briefly into English. It refers to the soft continuous crunching sound of the tyres compressing the grains of sand together as they roll over them.

PAKARRPA MIJILYIRRI

Mapal nganyjarranga ngungku kayinyu
ngayiny minturra kupalyangururra.
Pakarrpa mijilyirri kurlurlulu japarnu
parlparr warrukurla.

Kanyinpila yankurri puluu,
ngurra yangka-yangkarnintangu.
Yankurrilu warntarla wurtarla parrkaya parnirnu,
kalyangku murli-murli marnu.

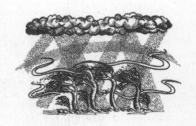

MORNING CYCLONE

It came at the right time for us, at daybreak,
we were awake after being asleep.[1]
It has covered the black night sky with red dust.

We've got this powerful blow here,
the countryside is being violently shaken.
Violently it has stripped the leaves
from the tops of the trees,
spinning around in the one place.

[1] The implication of the first sentence is that it is better to have a cyclone come in daylight than in darkness, and better to be fully awake, not groggy with being woken suddenly from deep sleep.

KANYINPILA YINJIN NGALANYA YANKURRI

Kanyinpila yinjin ngalanya
yankurri nganyjakapu kurtintangu.
Paka yirri kanimparrangururla
yulungkuya nganta marnu.

Malyarnu muku-mukuyinyu.
Parta pintalyirra jajarrarra nyinpa para!
Kuupukarta yankurri yinjin
nganyja yata jananyuru lapal wanyjarnanyurulu.

124

CATERPILLAR TRACTOR

Let's keep this energetic tractor
cutting down the sand.
That plucky (thing)
is knocking down the steep bank.

Slowly you backed back.
You've got a really huge mound for it to deal with!
That energetic tractor with the scoop
is pushing the sand and levelling it.

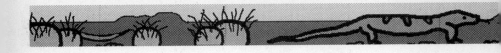

WANNGIRRIMANNYA

Kanji para wilyparr pungarnu,
yarlarrku wakartayinyjangurra.
'Palanya wanyaparri man puluu,
warnta ngurrumara!'

Yangkarla yangka-yangka marnu muurrkarralu,
murlungka kankarni jurta paarn marnu,
wanngirrimannya.

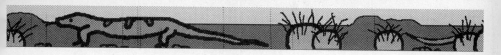

STORM HERALDING A CYCLONE

That storm on the side[1]
is heading on a detour,
the cyclone is curving round to
join up with it.[2]
'Listen to that blow,
it's an unstoppable tree smasher!'[3]

The house was flimsy
and the howling wind and rain shook the lot!
The wind slammed onto the rooftop,
the full force of the storm.

---

[1] The storm referred to in verse 1 is an inland one, but is recognised as being an outlier from a cyclone out over the ocean, beyond the horizon. Both the storm and the cyclone are heading westwards, but are expected to curve around and join up later. The phrase *wilyparr pungarnu* (referring to the storm) is an idiomatic use, literally 'hitting a detour'.

[2] The phrase *yarlarrku wakartayinyjangurra* (referring to the cyclone curving) is a hunting term for detouring around one's prey, to ambush it a bit further on.

[3] In the shaky hut, one person says to the other in fear, 'Listen to that wind! It's an unstoppable tree smasher!' (that is, it's a really powerful one).

JURTA PUPUPUKARRA WILYILA

Wanyjakalu palanyarla ngurnti yulayinyu?
Yiju para kana-kana manpila yirra nyanyjarrirra!

Palkaya ngali palu yumpukapungura.
Jurtarla murru marnu, kalya jaman pinanyurulu.

Yarlukarra warrarn ngurru
marnu wirntarntu murtilyarrangulu.
Parlparrpa waran marnu jurru-jurruralu.

Jurta pupupukarra wilyila,
palanya nyaarr warninyuru.
Jila wurntu jarturtu ngarlinymarra
ngarnkarra pakurta.

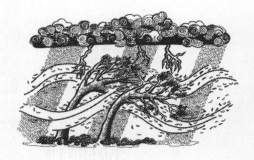

VIOLENT STORM

Where is that rumble announcing itself?
Look! Look out east at that
row of cliffs all equal size and shape![1]

I wonder how we'll fare
with that curse-loaded storm.[2]
It made it very windy,
with its continuous flashing.

It broke the country in half[3]
with its moving across,
covered it with its snakelike clouds.

Wind rushing from the east,
that sound of rushing wind and falling rain.
The whole cabbage tree gum is leaning,
almost uprooted.
Sadly its beautiful canopy
is now just a heap of debris.

[1] A reference to a baseline of clouds with several cumulus structures building up from it, evenly spaced and of even height.

[2] Implying that someone somewhere has worked magic to send this storm to cause trouble for a person or group (not necessarily including the song's composer).

[3] The main cloudbank's leading edge was straight, dividing the sky into clouded versus clear.

YARRKA KALYA KARLINY PUNTU-PUNTUYINYU

Yarrka kalya karliny puntu-puntuyinyu.
Ngurra yurnu jarnanyuru.
Kuntu-kuntu jakaly warninyu partulyayi
mangarrmarnarra kankaranguru.

Kurlurlu murli-murli marnu
purra wurla-wurla yankurrilu.
Murlinykurnu jarna purrpilu.
Wirnta, punkurirri, nganil ngayinyu,
pulyurru juntu wakanirnu.

Kanarni ngantaly-ngantaly marnu,
wurtarrinyuru,
jampa kanyinpila Jalyurnmalu,
warnta yalyu parlparr manyimara.

THE PLANE IS DESCENDING WHILE STILL A LONG WAY BACK

As he returns[1] he starts descending
from a long way back.
Now he is lining up with the airstrip.
The big bird has landed comfortably from above.

He makes the dust spin
with the propeller's rapid turbulence,
he scoops it up and throws it
in the opposite direction.
Crosswind, things sticking out,
he has started to move,
he turns straight into the wind.

The exhaust pipes underneath are throbbing,
he is standing there,
only holding it for a short time
at Roebourne airstrip,
that shiny sky-travelling expert.

---

[1] The composer knows that this plane (a DC-3?) landed at Roebourne on its
outward journey, and is now about to land there again on its way back to Perth.

KANYINJARRA! PIRRJARTA PARTA KALYA!

Kanyinjarra! Pirrjarta parta kalya!
Nyanta maananyuru.
Nyangu yila wurtarriya yirtinykarra,
yurlu partara Yurlumpurrngumalu.

Ngarnil jinarra panalu yarrkapirtimpuli.
Taya nyaarr marayan jurntika nyarru jipantangu.

Jinanyjurr Pinyarri jinyji parta,
nyayiya partangka kurlurlu Pirarrpurimalu.
Ngantu ngani marri pananya
pirralya yananyjangu Wirlurrkapumalu.

LOOK! YET ANOTHER LOT OF VEHICLES![1]

Look! Yet another lot of vehicles!
They keep on coming this way.
Maybe that convoy will stand in rows
somewhere here for a while,
maybe camp a while right here
at Yurlumpurrngunya.

They came from a long way
and they're not stopping here,
they're moving past.
The tyres make a loud noise
as they accelerate round the bend.

They're bypassing Pinyarri,
there's another cloud of bulldust
over there at Pirarrpuri.
I wonder who is watching this huge mob
as they go past Wirlurrkapu.[2]

[1] This song is about a World War Two army convoy coming up from Marble Bar
along the Great Northern Highway through De Grey Station, towards the North West
Coastal Highway. (In those days that was some ten kilometres nearer to the coast than
it now is). Two men (one of them the composer, the other Sandy's older brother) were
camped at Yurlumpurrngunya to fix a windmill when they saw this convoy, and the
composer immortalised it.

[2] The composer cannot see Wirlurrkapunya from where he is, but reckons the leading
trucks must be going past there by now.

YARALYPAMARRA

Parta ngaja nyinu ngungku jarri,
jajukarra, palangu, wulyulu.
Warrarnpa martupirri
jinyji pinyan, Yaralypamarralu!

Kurlurlu marnakarti winyja purlkayinyu.
Pirrjartarri murti kanyjilinypayi
karliny marraparra.

Partangka nyinpa wanangka
martupirringura pipurru,
murtuka jarna yiju Nimakalu jipan.

YARALYPAMARRA [1]

I'm visualising it, it's a long way for you,
that way, westwards. [2]
Over the hills and dales
you'll gobble up the stages, Yaralypamarra!

You are throwing away the dust behind you,
it is billowing upwards.
The vehicle is humming, speeding, swooping,
eagerly returning on the homeward journey.

You've got a long stage
across the valleys without a stop,
the car's back (is receding from us)
as you drive eastwards, Nimaka. [3]

[1] This is a secondary name of the man the song is about.

[2] Referring to the first stage of the trip, westwards some eighty kilometres to Port Hedland from De Grey Station. The traveller is actually from Wallal Downs, some 170 kilometres east of De Grey Station, so has a very long return trip ahead of him.

[3] This is actually a secondary name of the composer, not of his subject, Yaralypa, but these two men were *nyaparukarra*, that is, they shared the same primary name, which would be secret, known only to a very few, and very rarely used. In those circumstances all who knew the two people and knew that they shared the secret name (without the speakers themselves necessarily knowing what that secret name was), were free to use a secondary name of either of the two to refer to either one of them. Thus in this verse the composer used his own secondary name, Nimaka, not his subject's secondary name, to refer to the driver, because the two men shared the same primary name.

Kanturrpamarra

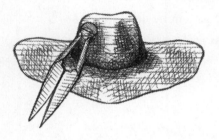

Kanturrpamarra was a stockman at De Grey Station. He spent some time travelling back and forth between De Grey Station and Port Hedland. He used to work around town, probably in the slaughter yards, with his younger cousin Wapirrku.

MARTUNKURAKARNI

Nganya nyurra wii mayirnta martunkurakarni.
Ngaya mirta purralyakura wangka kurilkura.
Yarlingkulpa wangka jilykari juntu marnanyuru.
Pikurrilu muwarr jiparnu ngaru marrangura.

TO THE ISLAND [1]

You were taking me over to the island. [2]
I don't talk Booby language. [3]
Oystercatchers repeatedly have to tell news.
Bad news makes them talk all along the coast. [4]

[1] This song is a classic example of the use of metaphor to convey indirectly what every Aboriginal person in the Pilbara in those days would have known to be the real message of the song.

[2] The composer presumably was taken as a patient to a VD prison on an isolated island. (Finucane Island near Port Hedland was used for a while as a holding camp; later such patients were taken to Dorre or Bernier Islands, out from Carnarvon.)

[3] Those islands were 'for the birds', considered not fit for human beings.

[4] There was a widespread belief along the Pilbara coast that a lone oystercatcher in flight (as distinct from a flock of them) was the bearer of bad news, such as the death of someone. The deaths of VD patients caused these birds to travel along the coast with the news. This reflects the gloom felt about the VD prisons, but the composer himself survived, and returned to De Grey Station; though he was dead by the time Alexander Brown learned this song there as a youth.

Pirarrarna Makanykarra

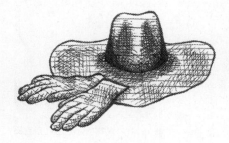

Pirarrarna Makanykarra was a stockman on De Grey
Station and Shaw River Station. He also did fencing and
post cutting. He spent most time at the Shaw River camp.
He joined the 1946 strike and passed away in the 1950s.

PAKARR NGARRARANGURA

Wiyil nguru-nguruyinyu Kurrumalu yarlurnangura,
wiyil nguru-nguruyinyu Kurrumalu
Mukurlirtimarrangu.

Wijilkapu mirlka mintu-minturri,
wijilkapu Mukurlirtimarrangu.

Ngaparra pirangarra wakarnirnu,
yanyararra wakin wika-wikarri.

WAGON BOGGED [1]

The wheels have sunk halfway at De Grey,
the wheels have sunk halfway at De Grey for
Donkey Charlie.[2]

At the whistle all heads jerk up,
at the whistle from Donkey Charlie.

In line abreast they wheeled,
it's going well, the wagon is beginning to move.

[1] Donkey teams pulling huge wagons with iron-rimmed wheels were used a lot in the Pilbara before motor vehicles came on the scene. This wagon had become bogged in the soft sand while crossing the dry bed of the De Grey River, right at Kurrunya, where the homestead is.

[2] The driver of the donkey team.

JAPARTA

Partangka murnmurlkurru ngunyi kuwanangura,
Partangka murnmurlkurru ngunyi Nyapirimarrangu
nyinu.

Ngarnkarra kamantangu wamu karri,
Ngarnkarra kamantangu nyinu Minngarimarra.

Jurta ngalparralu wurnkarra paja wakarninmara,
Jurta ngalparralu Pirarranangu.

Parnti ngarlinymarra jinkarrikarti,
Parnti ngarlinymarra Pirntiyimarrangu nyinu.

MUSTERING [1]

Another billowing cloud of smoke at that corner,
Another billowing cloud of smoke
where you are, Nyapiri.

The debris [2] will be burnt in flame and smoke,
The debris will be burnt where you are, Minngari.

Let the wind coming side-on
turn the dangerous blaze,
The side-on wind where you are, Pirarrarna.

The smoke is bent over in a line above the horizon,
The smoke is bent over where you are, Pirntiyi.

[1] Low-intensity 'firestick farming' is regularly used by pastoralists in spinifex and low scrub country in the Pilbara region to force the sheep or cattle out to where they can be more readily mustered and taken to stockyards. Here four men spaced out are lighting a long thin line of fire for that purpose.

[2] Dense heaps of accumulated debris, such as dead roly-poly bushes banked up against a scrub line, or flotsam left by a flood along the banks of a dry creek bed, burn fiercely.

WARNTARRA JAARNANYURU

Wanparr wangararri Pirrpawarnala,
wanparr wangararri warntarra jaarnanyuru.

Malyarnu jangku parirr mayangkarrangu para,
malyarnu jangku parirr Nyiwirringu.

THE TWO AXEMEN

Pirrpawarna is vigorously busy,
vigorously busy chopping trees.[1]

Nyiwirringu's hands are swinging slowly,
easily, powerfully,
his is a slow easy hand.[2]

[1] The two men are cutting fence posts.

[2] Whereas Pirrpawarna (a white man) is chopping rapidly, ineffectively, Nyiwirringu (an Aboriginal man) is swinging his axe slowly, but much more effectively. The implication is that by the end of the day he will have cut many more posts than Pirrpawarna.

Mingkarlajirri

Mingkarlajirri did mustering on the De Grey Station.
He was a nephew for Wapirrku and Kanturrpamarra.
He died in the late 1920s.

YUMPUKAPU

Yumpukapu ngalinga manta-mantarri,
wanangkangu pulala yirra wanyjarri.

Palkaya ngali palu purra wurla-wurlangura?
Jurta pirrimantangura wilyilangura.

Jukanykarti ngajapa wanyaparri man.
Maya karliny pulala paja wanyjarri.

THE CURSE [1]

That curse-loaded thing is hanging around us,
the rain and dust storm
is putting out a line of cloud.

I wonder how we are going to manage
this gusty turbulent wind.
The easterly wind is starting to build up.

Listen to this strong wind!
It is viciously hitting us from the other direction.

[1] 'Curse' is perhaps too strong a translation. *Yumpu* has to do with someone manipulating the environment or circumstances by magic so as to make things hard for someone, but not necessarily so as to kill them. This hardship may be intended to punish someone for misbehaviour, or to get revenge on them for some real or perceived personal injury.

WURLANYALU NGANYJARRANGA JURTA MURRU MARRI

Wurlanyalu nganyjarranga jurta murru marri,
jayin ngarnka wirti kanyin yinta ngurraralu.

Karlka-karlka ngapurlarnu ngarningkajarra.
Pampanurra nganunga — kura pirnanyuru.

THE MARBLE BAR POOL SPIRIT IS RELEASING A FLOOD [1]

The Marble Bar pool is releasing the wind for us,
the Water Snake [2] is poised to let the water go.

All the gullies are overflowing,
backing up, bank to bank
because of me — a stranger
— he doesn't want to recognise me. [3]

[1] In almost all of the songs in this collection, Alexander Brown knew the composers personally, and in many cases he remembers when they were composed, and the situations that prompted them. However, this one is older again. It is not known when this song was composed, but the composer (who would have been a 'mother's brother' for Sandy) died before 1920.

[2] Water Snake: Literally, 'waterhole local-inhabitant'.

[3] The implication is that the composer of this song is the cause of all this water, because he is a stranger. If he were a local, the spirit water snake would not have caused the excessive flooding.

WANAKURRU JURILIYANYA

Wurla-wurla parnngarra nyinta,
wurla-wurla pala nyinu.

Jinyji parta jinarra mari
wanakurru Juriliyanya.

Nyankamarra jurrkul jarnanyuru mari
nyaarr puru jurtintiyan.

HUGE AUSTRALIA [1]

You are tossing away the turbulence,
that's your spray there.[2]

It's another stage on your long journey,[3]
truly huge *Australia*.

Heading steadily away in a straight line,
truly your noise is covered by the sound of
the outgoing tide,[4]
as you disappear into the distance.

[1] This song was inspired by the sight of HMAS *Australia* departing, after picking up troops bound for World War One.

[2] The ship was too large to come right into the port across the sandbar that blocked the channel in those days, thus the ship could only be seen from the huge propellers. The troops had to be ferried out to embark.

[3] The composer knew that the ship was on a long journey, on which Port Hedland was only one port of call.

[4] Being at a distance also meant that the sound of the waves along the shore was enough to drown out the sound of the ship's engines as it departed in a direct line away from the shore.

Waparla Pananykarra

Waparla Pananykarra was Sandy Brown's brother. He started as a stockman on De Grey Station, before switching to repairing and building windmills. He also worked with the well sinkers. He left the station during the 1946 strike but went back with improved conditions in the 1960s and '70s. He later shared his time between Yandeyarra and 12 Mile just on the outskirts of Port Hedland. He passed away in Port Hedland in 1995. His two sisters, Susie and Betty, are still alive.

PAMPANU KARRIPULA NGANYA

Pampanu nganya.
Karripula para yintarra, ngani malyartara.
Warlumartari ngajapa juntu
marripula yinta Kunmayirtingkanya.

Manyjangurra nganu papa munka-munkarriyan,
kura pirnanyuru,
yinta ngurraralu nganya karrkuru
mampul pulyarr marnu!

YOU TWO TAKE ME AROUND, I'M A STRANGER HERE

I'm a stranger here.
You two take me to that waterhole, I'm ready to see it.
Those two are telling me
Kunmayirtingkanya is a dangerous waterhole.

He's disturbing the water because I'm a stranger,
he is disowning me,
the resident water snake has smelled
my underarm odour, for sure!

PIRTUNYA YINTA NGANU KUJUNGURRUNGURA

Nyumpalu nganya kalyurniyinyu,
yurtarra yurri jalyartara,
kalya yirntarra ngunparranikura.

Wataku, nganya jurni nyanpula,
yarrkakapumpuli,
puriyawalirnu ngaya kanimparrakapu.

Pirtunya yinta nganu kujungurrungura,
kurlkurarrakurrukapu ngaya ngarumarrakapu.

Jirnu-jirnura panalu ngarta yintakapu nganu.
Warrukarti nyarraya malkunti katakurrukapu.

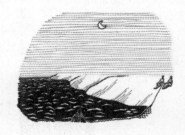

MY COUNTRY IS PIRTUNYA, ON THE COAST

You two called me, ready to go net fishing,
   in order to stumble around all night.[1]

It doesn't matter, you can laugh at me,
   I come from far away, up north.

My clan country[2] is Pirtunya,[3] on the coast.
It has lots of beach spinifex, and lots of sandy beach.

Those jirnu-jirnura spirit-beings,
   they come from my country.
They walk around all night in the thick scrub.

---

[1] He had been wading around in the water in the dark, often finding it hard to keep his balance because of the uneven bottom, stumbling over logs and debris in a part of the river he was not familiar with, upstream from his country, while the two women were holding the other end of the net, safe and dry, up on the bank!

[2] The composer's mother's clan's country ran from Walyparn Pool out to the mouth of the De Grey River. His father's country was around the mouth of Pardoo Creek, hence the clan name by which he was usually known, Pananykarra, the name of the area around Cape Keraudren.

[3] The English name for Pirtunya, west of the mouth of the De Grey, is Redbank. That name has been avoided in this translation because there is another area much better known by that name, near Port Hedland, and most people nowadays, being unaware of the one near the De Grey mouth, would incorrectly assume that the one near Port Hedland was the one referred to.

PALKAYA NYINPA PARA NGURRA PARRANYKU

Ngurntirri jipantangu,
yinjin malyarnu murli-murlirriyan wurtarrinyuru,
yumpukapu nganil marrapa jarna wulyulu.

Palkaya nyinpa para ngurra parranyku,
jinyjipilyartara mapalyanyangka jarurrany.
Jangku murru mantangu Laanturupa ngurra yarrkarra.

Jarriyirti kankalakarta,
jarrari waru kayinyu pirrpangka.
Kuntu kaman mulya wulyulu yarrkawanti Yirrmaringu.

I WONDER HOW YOU ARE GOING TO FARE ON THIS LONG TRIP

It's been started up,
the engine is turning over slowly
while it's standing there,
eager to head westwards
because of important business.

I wonder how you will fare on the long trip,
ready to do the stretch easily after sunset.
Let the Landrover go, heading for the far country.

Bright light rising and falling,
lights glowing brightly.
Teddy Allen is taking it skilfully,
nose westwards for the long trip.

YARRKA MURRI NGAJA NGUNGKU JARRI NYINU MAPURLPA

Yarrka murri ngaja ngungku jarri nyinu,
Mapurlpa pirringkarra nganilku,
kupalyayanyangku ngurra
marrany marnu palangu yiju.

Pilurru murti ngayinyjangu wapu jumpin,
palangu, kanimparra.
Yarrkapirti yinjin karnmartayinyjangu.
Kuntu kaman, Kariwarna!

I'M THINKING MARBLE BAR'S A LONG WAY AWAY FOR YOU

I'm thinking it's a very long way for you,
to go to Marble Bar in the afternoon.
No sleep, traversing the distance freely
out that way, eastwards.

While it's heading that way, urge it on,
that way, on the downhill run.
After coming a long way the engine
is really warming up now.
Treat it carefully, Peter Coppin.

The composer is concerned for his friend, who has a long drive ahead of him.

NGURNTIRRI JIPANTANGU NGUNTUNTU KARRIYAN

Wiyilta ngurntirri jipantangu,
nguntutu karriyan.
Nyayila pananya riyil-riyil yayin
pirli jan wiyiltakartangku.

Marangka palarr karra mantangura
nyintapa jirntakurru marnu.
Wiyilta ngurntirri pumarr karriyan
marntarra pirli jarnanyuru.

Layin junturarrangka yayin wanyjantangu.
Warnta pukarrmaru, yirtinykarra
wanyjantangu Wamiyingungu.

IT'S STANDING STILL AFTER THE MOTOR HAS BEEN STARTED UP

The welder has been started up,
it's stationary.
He will put holes in these iron rails [1]
with the welder.

While being held firmly in your hand
it makes streams of sparks.
The welder noise roars
as the holes are made in the steel.

The lengths of iron have been left
standing up in a straight line.
The wooden railings are complete,
joined up in their rows by Clancy McKenna. [2]

[1] A stockyard is under construction, with upright lengths of old railway line for posts and local timber for rails (probably cut from coolabah trees).
[2] The posts have now been put up in position, and the wooden railings fastened to them. The stockyard is completed.

PALKAYA NYINPA PALU

Palkaya nyinpa palu!
Palakarningurala jampirr-jampirr!
Nyinu yulu wurtarriyan
pilyparr ngumpalpunyjarri.

'Nyanta palu jakurr manpiya,
wayi jarrpinyamarta kiirtingura.'
Yankurri, kurtul!
Yata jantangu ngarlipurra Ngarlkapangungu.

168

I WONDER HOW YOU ARE GOING TO HANDLE HIM

I wonder how you are going to handle him![1]
He's a tough one!
He's standing gamely for you,
you can't hunt him away.

'You fellows coax him over this way,
see if he'll go through the gate.'[2]
He was lively, but he's finished!
He's been forced over onto his side
by Jack Coppin.

---

[1] The scene is a cattle yard, and the object of interest is a large and lively young long-horned bull, with its head lowered in a stubborn stance.

[2] From the large square yard the bull is manoeuvred through a gate into the small circular pen in which the animal is to be thrown and held down, ready for whatever treatment is planned, such as branding or castration.

Jawalya Pilu

Jawalya Pilu ran the mustering camp at De Grey Station.

NYANGKALA MURRI PANANYA PUNPARU PAJIRRI

Nyangkala murri pananya punparu pajirri.
Kupartu, nguurn marrinyuru, wanngarrka yartara.

Marlungulu purnu jakarl pirnu,
marna marlirri, wurany yanangkayan.

THE SICKNESS IS REALLY STRIKING THEM NOW [1]

The sickness is really striking [2] them now.
Moaning, every one flattened, lying down.

The maggots have hollowed their rear ends out,
buttocks tucked in, [3] going along cringed. [4]

---

[1] This song is a reference to blowfly strike and its debilitating effect on sheep.

[2] Literally 'eating them'.

[3] Their backs are humped, so that they have a 'tail-between-their-legs' appearance.

[4] The stance of a little dog being threatened by a much larger, bullying, one.

KURLURRUMARNUNYA

'Nyangu pananya kurtany jinyjarra
marirralu ngaparimalingka.
Palkaya ngalila panalu kariyakangura!'

'Palarr karramanpiya yurin marukayinyjangurra.'
Wurla-wurlalu nganyjarranya ngampurrjarli marnu.

Ngalparra juntu ngarnikarni,
karlkamurntungura,
ngalanya paja warninyuru kurlurrumarnunya.

RAGING FLOOD [1]

'We'll make them cross here,
those children, Cousin.
I wonder how we will fare with them,
in this ocean of water!'[2]

'You kids[3] hold tight to the reins,
on account of the horses rearing and plunging.'[4]
The turbulence really hassled us.

In line abreast we headed straight towards the bank,
even though the water was backed right up
into the tributary gullies,
in this dangerous tumbling raging flood.

---

[1] This song describes the crossing of the De Grey River when it was in flood in 1943, at the spot where the road bridge now is on the Great Northern Highway. It involved two adults, Jawalya and his male cousin, and their five children (who were therefore cousins to each other), plus a couple of dogs. Each child was riding a separate horse. Jawalya was the composer of this song, and one of the children was Sandy Brown, who transcribed this song fifty-three years later in 1996.

[2] In the normally dry riverbed there are many islands covered with small but dense bushes. These were now submerged. It was important to pick the crossing site carefully, and allow for sideways drift as the horses swam, lest the horses' legs tangle with any such bushes. The men therefore needed to aim for a spot on the other side where the bottom sloped up to the bank, while at the same time avoiding any vegetation en route that might tangle and trip the horses.

[3] They are not called children in the song (though they were that), being referred to instead by the kin term indicating their relationship to each other. See footnote 1.

[4] A reference to the way horses can swim with a 'slow-motion gallop' effect, resulting in a heaving motion rather than a smooth one.

PURLARN MIRNA NYINILA PANALALA

Purlarn mirna nyinila panalala
waju yajarinykarrangura.
Panalu yanangkayanpiya ngurrarra
yurnu jarnanyuru.

Ngunyi kalya panalu, pakangka wurruru,
jirrparnkalirri, pirntilirri wartarrangura.

STOP QUIET AWHILE FOR THEM

Be silent awhile for them as they march past.[1]
They are choosing a camp site.

There they are still, on the south bank,
firearms shouldered,
bayonets sticking up beyond their shoulders.

[1] A contingent of soldiers in Port Hedland in World War Two.

Jirlparurrumarra Piraparrjirri

Jirlparurrumarra Piraparrjirri was also known as 'Bobby Dazzler'. He did stockwork but was mostly an offsider to a well-sinking team. He was also an amateur boxer. He joined the strikers after 1946 but went back to station work with the improved conditions in the 1960s and '70s. He passed away there.

MAMPUL MURRI PANALU NYAYI NGARTA MANGKARRJARA

Mampul murri panalu nyayi ngarta mangkarrjara!
Wangarrinypa panalu nyayi yinji wirti-wirti.

Ngarti-ngarti jina marnu marnuwarralu nganu.
Palanya kukurnkarra!
Jirntiyarrangura ngurntirri karri.

Jirntu kanarlirlingurala wangka yulayinyu
manara yarra nganu pijirrirra munyjurnanguru!

TRULY THEIR LOUD NOISE KEEPS A MAN AWAKE

Truly these mosquitoes annoy me with their noise!
They are determined to pester me.

Mobs of them are tracking towards me
along the river bank.
Listen to that buzzing!
In the night-time quietness they are roaring.

In the pre-dawn darkness as they were going
their noise told me they had already
swallowed my blood!

NGUNTU PURNNGURAYINYU

Parta ngaja nyurrala ngurra ngani
marri ngurlparra-ngurlparra.
Jajukarra Wirlpirlpinya yirra wipiny ngarayan.

Palkaya ngaya palu.
Ngayiny kurturn-kurturn,
karral-karral, ngungku pakurta,
kuji jankanka puru.

Purlarn nyinila para, jantiwayirra,
piparra purnngurayinyjangurra.
Yurala-yurala ngarra maninyu.

Yinyja-yinyja, kupilya-kupilya, nguntu
purnngurayinyu.
Nyurrungkarti kanyarla.

Kartarlu nganyjarra;
karrkalypa maninguru mulya nganngarumani,
kangkuka nyininyuru.

THE FEVER IS ENVELOPING US

I am seeing the country differently,
you fellows, all hazy.
The cliffs at Wirlpirlpinya [1] faraway
are appearing and disappearing in my vision.

I'm uneasy about it.
My heart is beating fast,
I'm clumsy, feeling crook,
my legs are shaky.

Stay quiet on account of that sickness,
that enveloping fever.
It is increasing, spreading, rising.

Like dew, like fog, the flu is enveloping us.
The phlegm has started.

We are in a bad way;
from being happy we have lapsed into despair,
with our heads slumped on our knees.

---

[1] Wirlpirlpinya is much too far away to be seen from where the composer was at De Grey Station. It may be that he is referring to his inability to keep a visualisation of Wirlpirlpinya in his mind; in other words, he is unable to hold a thought clearly.

YANGKARL-YANGKARLKARRA! KURRUNYA YIRRIRRIKAPU!

Wanyjakalulu nganyjarranga
parlangkarna murru marri,
jukanyja yirtikurla para jarlurarrikurru
marnanyuru ngarramani?

Nguwalinypa nyaarra yampu ngajururr karri.
Ngannya-ngannya!
Wuntulypirnanyuru jurta purra wurlarri.

Karrpartinya ngarlu wukurrurru
wakatarri-wakatarrinyuru.
Martuwarra Pulyuwarinya jipalpintangu.

Pinpaka ngarramani karti yirrkaliji.
Kurrkarrka pipurru jananpirri. Wanngirrimannya!

Yirtirntirra wanya payila palu! Yangapintangura!
Yangkarl-yangkarlkarra! Kurrunya yirrirrikapu!

IT'S REALLY RATTLING! KURRUNYA IS SHAKING!

Where is the one who is sending this
weather change [1] for us,
skilfully blending in the increasing
wind with lots of rain?

The roar of a cyclonic wind is singing.
Crash! Crash! as the boughs snap.
The wind is whisking them away in its eddies.

The eye [2] of the cyclone is twisting and turning.
Somebody [3] started it up north,
Pulyuwarinya way.

The increasing lightning and storm noises
are coming towards us.
The wind force has doubled up without stopping.
The full force of the storm has hit us!

Listen to the shaking! And the rocking!
It's really working at rattling!
De Grey is shuddering!

[1] *Parlangkarna* refers to increasing temperature, usually with a hot wind.
[2] Literally stomach.
[3] A rainmaker is suspected of having started any unusually strong storm.

PUKAPANNYA

Warntaparri nguru-nguruya nganyjarranga
Pukapannyakapu!

Piparu, ngarramanimara, kurlurrumarnunya.

OUR POOR TREES ARE ALMOST SUBMERGED

Our poor trees from Pukapannya[1]
are almost fully submerged!

Flowing steadily, let it rise,[2]
this raging flood.

[1] Pukapannya is a small island covered with dense trees, near the bank of the De Grey River just below where the De Grey homestead stands. Kurrunya Pool is just downstream from it.

[2] The permissive suffix *–mara* often expresses an attitude of resignation; here it's not that the composer wants the flood to keep on rising, but that there is no way he can stop it.

Index of Song Titles